HUCKLEBERRY FINN

MARK TWAIN

Adapted by Dr. Marion Kimberly

GALLERY BOOKS
An Imprint of W. H. Smith Publishers Inc.
112 Madison Avenue
New York City 10016

© 1990 Ediciones B, S.A., Barcelona, Spain

This edition published 1991 by Gallery Books,
an imprint of W.H.Smith Publishers, Inc.,
112 Madison Avenue, New York, New York 10016

ISBN 0-8317-1460-3

Gallery Books are available for bulk purchase for sales
promotions and premium use. For details write or telephone
the Manager of Special Sales, W.H.Smith Publishers, Inc.,
112 Madison Avenue, New York, New York 10016. (212) 532-6600

Produced by Hawk Books Limited, London

Printed in Spain

Our story begins about 1850 in a little town in the American Midwest. It was a peaceful town on a river, a good place to grow up. Few people would have heard of it if not for...

One day there was a party at the school...

I'm going to speak to Judge Thatcher about those boys.

I think you should, Miss Dorothy.

One of the boys was Tom Sawyer. You must have heard of him.

Another was called Huck... Huck Finn, to be exact.

Time for supper, and then to bed.

Now, Mrs. Douglas? Do I have to go in? Oh, all right.

Jim was the third boy...

Aaaahhh...

Boy, life without any adventures is a big bore. First Tom started behaving and then Widow Douglas took Huck in and adopted him. Now I'm miserable. I feel like a fish in a barrel of rainwater!

Things have been pretty calm since their last tricks. We'll see just how long it lasts.

You're right, Miss Pattibush. Those boys...

The three boys were about to cause a lot of talk. It all started that very night...

Hey! That's Tom's password!

MEOW! MEEOWW!

MEEOW!

Minutes later...

Were you asleep? I thought so.

What's up, Tom?

The gang is all ready. They're waiting for us. Let's go.

Just a minute. We've got a gang, Tom? What are we going to do? Walk each other to school?

Of course not! You don't need a gang for that!

Look! There they are!

Hi, chief.

Listen you guys! Everyone has to take an oath. Swear with me that you'll keep our secrets, even if it means death. Are you all ready?

Wow! You are serious, aren't you, Tom?

Uh oh. It could be dangerous!

Cowards! Are you scared even before we start? Are you men or mice?

MEN!

Mice! I'm scared.

After they had all taken the oath . . .

I'm your leader. I name Joe Harper as second in command. In case he dies, Huck Finn is next in line.

Okay, but what are we going to do?

We'll do the things all brave gangs pledge themselves to do. We'll chase bandits, catch stagecoach robbers, and things like that.

That sounds like fun! When do we start?

The next day they set out to capture outlaws, but . . .

We've been here for hours, Tom. There aren't any bandits around here.

This is dumb! Nothing ever happens here!

They were wrong. A great adventure was just ahead of them.

Okay now, take it easy. We'll find some real danger. Just when we least expect it, bang! Now, let's go back to town, gang.

Later Huck and Tom . . .

Tom, I've got to ask Judge Thatcher about something important.

Gee, Huck, is it about the money he's keeping for us? Our reward for finding the robbers' loot?

Yes. I want him to help me make everybody think I haven't any money.

Are you afraid of something?

Well, in a way, Tom, yes. I don't know. I have a feeling. I'll see you later.

Later, at Judge Thatcher's house . . .

If that's all you want, relax my boy. If anybody asks me about it, I'll say you don't have a cent.

Thanks, Judge Thatcher.

Later that day, Huck's fear began to come true...

Are you in there, Mrs. Douglas? No. She must have gone shopping.

You weren't expecting your father, were you?

What? Pa!

Quite the gentleman, aren't you? Don't think much of your father, eh? Ha! Ha!

I understand. They tell me that you have a lot of money. Bet you got a big kick out of finding that loot!

No, I don't have a single dollar. That's the truth, Pa!

Don't lie to me! Take that!

Owww!

No use trying to get away. I'm going to keep you with me until you tell me where the money is.

No, let me go! Let me go!

Huck's attempts to escape were in vain. His father was a strong man and he forced Huck to go to a lonely cabin.

It's not going to be easy to get away from me, heh, heh, heh!

I'm telling you, Huck. You won't leave here until you promise to give me the money.

I've already told you, Pa. I don't have a cent!

You're lying again, you rascal! I know all about the money they gave you as a reward for finding the treasure of those thieves.

Listen! The boat whistle!

Three days passed. In town everyone was upset about Huck's disappearance.

Don't cry, Ma'am. Something mysterious has happened, but I'll bet Huck's alive.

Oh, why doesn't he let us know he's alive? What could have happened to him, Tom?

Sheriff! Is there any news about the boy?

Not a thing. More than likely he's just run off. I've told the shipping company about his disappearance, in case they want to look for him along the river.

Wait, I'm going to ask Tom Sawyer a few questions.

Not again, Sheriff! I've already told you I don't know where Huck Finn is. And Jim, the black boy, doesn't know either.

You're sure, Tom?

I've told you everything I know, Sheriff. I'm a man of honour! If Huck had gone on one of his adventures, he'd have told me. I know he would.

Which makes me believe, Sheriff, that Huck is in some kind of serious trouble. But I've got a strong feeling he's still alive.

Meanwhile, in the lonely cabin in the woods...

Hic... I'm going to celebrate in advance, Huck. Because I know you're about to tell me... hic... where that money is.

This is my chance! If I don't get away from Pa now, I never will!

What do you say to that, Huck?

Minutes later he was in the woods. Everything had gone much better than he had expected.

I'm sure that if he doesn't find me, he'll end up leaving town forever. So I've got to make him believe that I'm dead.

Uh oh! He must know that I've escaped!

But Huck was wrong...

Hic...I must have drunk more than I thought. Guess I'd better sober myself up.

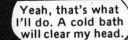

Yeah, that's what I'll do. A cold bath will clear my head.

But, the truth is, I can't even seem to stand up. Oh dear...

Thank goodness! He's finally passed out. Now's my chance.

Huck quickly went back to the cabin and . . .

When he wakes up, he'll think the cabin has been attacked and that bandits have taken me away with them.

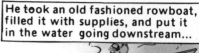

He took an old fashioned rowboat, filled it with supplies, and put it in the water going downstream...

I've got to make Pa believe that I'm dead. Then he'll go away for good and I can stay here.

Suddenly he heard a sound he couldn't mistake . . .

They must be shooting the cannon from a boat!

BOOM!

They're looking for me! Good! I want everyone to think I've been killed or captured by bandits. Then Pa will believe it and leave me alone.

Huck Finn had just about convinced everyone he was dead...

There's not a sign of anyone here, Captain.

All right. Let's go back. We'll tell the sheriff we couldn't find him anywhere.

And that night while Huck was sleeping peacefully in the woods . . .

Back in town...

Tom, anything new about Huck?

It's horrible, Jim. His father came and told the sheriff that Huck...that Huck must have been killed by bandits.

No, that can't be! But . . . what does his father have to do with all this, Tom?

Huck's Pa said they were on a hunting trip. That doesn't sound right to me, but the sheriff believes him.

The boat they sent out looking for Huck didn't find any sign of him. It's awful! How are we going to tell Mrs. Douglas?

And she loved him so much!

Tom, those people in New Orleans are trying to get me back. They want to make me a slave again. I've got to escape!

Good luck.

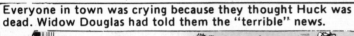
Everyone in town was crying because they thought Huck was dead. Widow Douglas had told them the "terrible" news.

Why did this have to happen to that little angel? And to think that I quarreled with him so much!

Calm down, Mrs. Douglas. The Lord will take care of him.

Oh, Huck! He was such a good boy.

Almost a little angel. A bit naughty, but a good boy.

Take care, Jim. We won't forget you!

Thanks, Tom. I won't forget you either.

Jim began running into the woods and didn't stop until it was dawn.

Ugh, I can't go any further. I need a little rest.

Hey, what's that noise?

Who...who goes there?

Nooooo!

Oh my gosh! Huck Finn! Get away from me! You're dead!

No! Get back! You're dead, Huck Finn!

What are you talking about, Jim? Why are you here?

A little later, after exploring the area, they found an abandoned cabin.

Let's go! It can be our hideout.

Jim was still scared, but he told Huck about what had happened.

So, they all think I'm dead. That's just what I wanted. Now Pa will go away and...

Good! You are all right, aren't you, Huck?

Jim had his own story to tell Huck. His former masters were trying to get him back and make him a slave again.

Aw, don't worry. From now on, you stay with me. I'll never betray you, Jim.

Thanks, Huck. I knew I could count on you as a friend.

Yeah, it does seem to be abandoned, Huck.

Look here, clothes, women's clothes and food...

Hey, not bad. And I'm hungry already.

What do you plan to do, Huck? Hide for the rest of your life? You're pretty young for that.

Nooo...No. As soon as I'm sure Pa's gone, I'll go back to town. Mrs. Douglas will be glad to see me.

How are you going to know your Pa is gone? One of us will have to go back and see...

You're right! I know! Tomorrow I'll disguise myself and go to town. People won't recognize me dressed in women's clothes.

The next day . . .

Ha! Ha! You sure look funny, Huck.

I'm going to one of the farms near town. The people have to go to town to shop. They'll know about Pa.

Huck approached a farmhouse...

I hope this works...

Good morning, Ma'am.

Oh, you surprised me, little girl!

It's not safe for you to be out alone after what's happened.

Why, what is wrong, Ma'am?

You really don't know? Young lady, people say that Huck Finn has been killed!

Oh, no! Really?

And the latest rumour is really horrifying! They say that Jim, the little black boy, must have killed him!

Ma'am! Huck Finn and Jim have always been close friends.

And now, little one, run on home and don't come back to these lonely parts. Today the sheriff and his deputy are going on a careful search.

Do you mean they're looking for Huck Finn's body? Maybe they should look for his father.

It was his father who reported Huck's disappearance. The poor man is so sad. He'd do anything to help find the boy.

I like that! Pa, unhappy because I'm missing! He just wants the money!

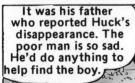

Odd little girl! Why would she say they should be looking for his father?

Jim! Jiiiimmm...

Quick, Jim! The sheriff is coming this way! Pa's still in town, and he's following the sheriff!

B...but Huck, look! We're going to have a storm. All our things are in the cabin!

Forget it. Let's go!

The storm turned out to be a bad one . . .

I can't go on, Huck. I'm really afraid of storms!

Look, a boat! That's the best way to get us out of here once and for all, Jim

Are you going to leave in this storm?

Minutes later . . .

We're going to wreck, Huck! We're going to wreck!

Hang on, Jim! Look over there!

A boat! It must have run aground!

We're going to crash, too!

Easy! It's a risk, but we'll be safer in this boat than...

A little later...

Watch out!

Follow me, Jim!

The boat's in good condition, but there's not much room.

Let's go!

Huck and Jim quickly left the boat that was aground . . .

Hurry up, row! If we don't, we're goners!

Meanwhile, in the town, people were growing more concerned about Huck's disappearance. His father told the sheriff...

You see, Sheriff, when I got back to the cabin, the boy wasn't there. I'm sure he was carried off by robbers.

Huck's father kept quiet about being drunk when Huck disappeared. And of course he didn't tell anyone that he really wanted to get Huck's money.

Do you believe the boy was killed?

Sheriff, I don't even want to think about that!

What were you and Huck doing in that cabin? Huck lives with Widow Douglas who adopted him.

The boy wanted to spend some time with me in the woods.

He also didn't mention that he had taken Huck from the Widow's house by force! Huck had been his prisoner in the cabin!

All right. But for now, I advise you not to leave town until we find out exactly what happened.

I won't, Sheriff...

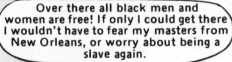

Hmm, I don't like the direction this thing is taking. I think I'd better tone it down and forget about Huck's money.

Two days later, Huck and Jim pulled up to a pier . . .

Look, at least we've come as far as Illinois.

But I want to get to the northern part. In the north I can be a free citizen.

Over there all black men and women are free! If only I could get there I wouldn't have to fear my masters from New Orleans, or worry about being a slave again.

Later, as Huck prepared to go ashore . . .

You stay here. I'll go and see where we are. Don't let anyone see you. I'll be as quick as I can.

Just a minute, young man. Is there a slave in that boat with you?

Uh, what did you say, sir?

Slave? Sir, we're in trouble. What's happened is...is that...we're sick.

And just what is the matter?

Huck was afraid that the men would go to the boat and see that Jim was a runaway slave. So he told them...

We have...it's... SMALLPOX!

GOOD LORD!

He's so calm! It's horrible!

Smallpox! Get away from them!

Huck hurried back to the boat and...

Let's go, Jim. We've got to go upriver. We're still in the South. Those men I saw are going around looking for runaway slaves.

Two days later, after some tough going...

We'd better dock the boat here. Our food is gone. I just can't row on an empty stomach.

Wait right here, Jim. I hope we have better luck this time.

We could sure use some good luck, Huck.

I'll knock on the door of the first house I see. I'm really hungry. Maybe they'll give me something.

So he did...

Good day. I'm sorry to bother you but I'm a poor orphan.

Oh . . . an orphan! Wait here a minute.

There is a poor orphan outside, sir. He looks as if he were half dead, poor thing.

That's a shame.

Bring him in and give him something to eat.

Come in, boy. My people will be kind to you.

Tell me, please. Are we in the North or South? Do you know what I mean?

In the South. Boy, you are white, you are safe here.

Thank you. I did not know...

Oh, but he really is just a poor boy!

And what a hungry look he has. Take him to the kitchen, Susan.

Yes, Master. Right away.

To Huck, it all seemed to be a happy dream. Soon he would wake up . . .

Why are you showing me all this good food?

Come on now. Serve yourself, young man. Eat as much as you like.

Huck was so hungry he dove right in and . . .

Could I take some of this to my poor dog? It's been two weeks since he had a mouthful.

Of course you can. I'll wrap up some bones so your dog can have a good meal.

The miserable traitor! Look at him eating while I'm here starving!

Here, these are for your dog.

Thank you very much.

Jim's not going to like a pile of bones.

Could I...My dog would just love this. There seems to be more than enough in this house...

Well, I declare! alright, boy, it's yours.

Thanks again. Thanks a lot!

Thanks . . .

Jim, look what I've got!

Know something, Huck? For a second there, I thought you'd deserted me!

You saw me eating, huh?

Later...

We're heading South, Jim. It's not that I'm afraid I'll run into my father. But we can't go back that way.

They were about to set off again...

Boys! Wait just a minute, please.

Now you can shove off, young man.

Hurry! The whole town is chasing us!

We're both famous actors from the London theater. I'm David Garrick, this is Edmund Kean.

We just presented the play, Hamlet, in this town.

Rude hicks! They didn't understand a word of the play. They threatened to hang us!

That doesn't mean we have to take you on board, gentlemen. Please do us a favour and get off.

You young rascal! You're going to take us down the river to the next town. If you don't...

Huck soon realized that the two men were not talking or acting in a reasonable manner...

We, the marvellous Garrick and Kean, of worldwide fame, will leave the public open-mouthed in admiration of our performances . . .

The balcony scene from Romeo and Juliet!

What a couple of screwballs! Those two are really crazy!

Then let's get away from them as fast as we can!

Getting away wasn't going to be easy. It was dawn when they got to the next town.

You two are smart, wide-awake boys. You will be part of our great theatre company!

Awake? I'm so tired I'm falling asleep on my feet.

Oh boy, just what we needed!

You will play the role of Juliet. I, of course, will be Romeo.

But I'm a man. I can't play the part of a girl. No one would believe me.

But Garrick knew just what he wanted to do, and the boys had no choice . . .

We have five dollars left. We'll rent costumes. We'll make this the finest performance ever given.

Now, we are going to put your face to work! The great David Garrick is going to turn you into an actor!

You understand? They'll work hard and we'll double our usual earnings.

And so, that very night . . .

SHAKESPEAREAN REVIVAL!
One night only!
Starring
David Garrick and Edmund Kean
of London in
The balcony scene-Romeo and Juliet
The thrilling duel of
Richard the Lionhearted
Admission 25 cents-children 10 cents

Huck was very unhappy in his role as Juliet and he could see that his real troubles were just beginning.

We've got to get away from these two madmen before it's too late!

Sure, Huck. But how? They never take their eyes off us!

The boy can't play Juliet without practising.

Stop bothering me, Kean. Why do you want to rehearse? The play will do nothing more than start. Ha, ha, ha!

Why concern yourself with the performance? We'll never finish the play. The people will run us out of town, as usual. Ha! Ha! Ha!

The moment came for the play to begin . . .

Ladies and gentlemen, the first act is about to begin. Please be quiet. We hope you will enjoy the show.

Juliet! Sweet Juliet of my heart. Are you really there?

Please pay me to see the show, ladies and gentlemen. Ah, thank you very much. Thank you...

Soon . . .

Hmmm...I'm sure ...I know that "little girl."

Of course! It is, it's Huck, the godchild of Widow Douglas. Huck, boy!

Huck was afraid of being recognized here in the town where his father had once lived.

Oh, you're wrong, Ma'am. I'm a girl. Can't you see it?

Juliet, you are a light that shines from the heavens above.

Ma'am, I'm a young girl. I don't know anything about this boy, Huck.

How strange! I'm not sure that's the truth.

Hmm. Well, it's easy to find out.

You are right. Let us go back stage and talk to this girl, if she is really a girl.

So they did . . .

This way ladies. Follow me.

What are you doing, ladies?

Owwww!

Let's get out of here, Jim!

Come on, Huck. RUN!

I'm telling you, that's no girl. It's the godson of a friend of mine in a neighbouring town!

Enough! Please go back to your seat and let the play go on.

But it was already too late for that, since . . .

Garrick, they're gone! The boys have escaped!

This has been nothing more than a poor excuse to get money from us!

You're right!

CHEATERS! THIEVES!

Give us our money back!

Let's hang them!

Wait a second, Jim!

But why? They're right behind us!

Now we have them!

Everyone in town is headed this way, Huck. They'll catch us, too.

I'll take care of that, Jim. You watch these two robbers.

Wait! Let me tell you what happened. My friend and I are innocent.

What nonsense!

All four of you got together to cheat us!

Luckily for Huck and Jim, the sheriff showed up just then, so Huck was able to tell the whole story . . .

And that's it, sir. We were the ones in danger because those men forced us to go with them. We couldn't get away.

Later, Garrick and Kean gave up. They admitted that Huck had been telling the truth, so that . . .

Okay, fellows. Get going. I think a good rest in jail will do you good. This town doesn't need any more trouble.

It was dawn the next day when . . .

I'm glad that's over! Now what shall we do with these costumes?

I'm afraid we'll never get our own clothes back. They were probably burned. What a mess!

Well, at least you're dressed as a boy. But me, dressed up as Juliet . . .

Wait, I have an idea . . .

We're just going to have to take those old clothes over there. After all, we need them much more than anyone else.

Moments later . . .

Footsteps! Who is it? Answer me!

Didn't you hear me? Is that you, Joe?

Eh? It's not possible...

Oh, it's my niece, Polly. When did you get here? I'm so glad . . .

She's confused me with someone else. What'll I do now.

But at that point Huck couldn't do anything but play along because . . . Oh, honey, you can't travel alone around here. Take this stick. Your cousin Joe should be here soon. Do come into the house with me.

Of course, Auntie.

Oh boy, why did I come to the home of such a nearsighted lady?

Well, how quiet you've become, Polly. Come on, tell me, how's your grandmother?

Fine, she's fine, Auntie.

I hope Joe is as nearsighted as she is.

Oh my gosh! I wonder what's keeping Huck.

Walking to the house...

This is the most romantic book I've ever read in my life!

The Capulets and the Montagues! There aren't any people like that anymore, no sir!

Oh, who's that? I wonder, am I seeing things? No, I'm not! Boy!

A real live flesh and blood Capulet!

Uh, oh!

Wait! Please, I want to talk to you!

Helllp! Helllp!

Listen, Polly. Did you hear a scream? Someone's in danger!

I'll see!

Wait here, I'll take a look...

Jim!

Let's go, Huck! Let's get out of here!

Noooo!

A Capulet fleeing, with the lovely Juliet . . .

I told you, Huck. I didn't like that "scene" at all.

Joe, here you are. Did you see Polly?

I haven't seen Polly or anything else! I can't eat so many beans. They give me nightmares!

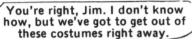

You're right, Jim. I don't know how, but we've got to get out of these costumes right away.

Agreed!

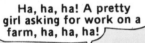

Maybe we could do some work and be paid in clothes.

Think so? Huck, who would hire us in these getups?

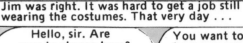

Jim was right. It was hard to get a job still wearing the costumes. That very day . . .

Hello, sir. Are you in charge here? We're looking for work, and...

You want to work here, young lady?

Ha, ha, ha! A pretty girl asking for work on a farm, ha, ha, ha!

That's enough! I'm not a young girl, I'm a man just like you.

I don't like this at all, Huck.

Look! Look at how I can work! Do you think a girl would be able to do this?

Wow!

For reasons that don't really matter, we're wearing these crazy clothes. We'll do any work you want in exchange for some proper clothes.

And so a few hours later . . .

Finally, old pal. This is more like it.

Heck, with all the trouble we've had, I almost forgot about Mrs. Douglas and Pa. I hope he's left town, Jim!

If he has, you could go home. But remember, back home they think you're dead, Huck.

Don't forget that, Huck. They have no reason to believe you are alive.

I know. And you've got to remember that your old master is looking for you. Be very careful, Jim!

Huck barely finished speaking when a man appeared...

Are you in charge here? Maybe you can give me some information about a certain black boy. I've been looking for him for days...

I went to his home, but they don't know where he is. Maybe he's in this part of the country.

Oh Lord! It's my master from New Orleans, Huck! I'm lost!

Oh, no!

He hasn't seen you yet. Run, Jim, run!

There! That's the boy! He won't escape again!

Unfortunately, Jim's master was right. Moments later . . .

So you want to make trouble again? Well, this time there won't be any mercy for you.

Oh, no! Let me go, please!

Poor Jim! If only there was something I could do for him.

Just then, Huck heard a voice over his shoulder, a very familiar voice . . .

You're wrong, Huck. We can find a way to help Jim.

Tom! Tom Sawyer!

Shhh! Don't shout, Huck!

I've been following Jim's old master. He was in town for days, looking for Jim. Then when I saw you, I thought I'd faint from fright! Like everyone else, I thought you were dead, Huck.

Well you see, I'm not! What's happening in town? Has Pa left yet?

Poor Mrs. Douglas has already had three funeral services for you, Huck, to save your soul. And your father finally left town when you didn't show up. No one knows where he's gone.

Meanwhile...
Goodbye, I'm taking this boy with me since he belongs to my family.

I'm sorry, Jim. Good luck.

Careful, don't let that slaver see you. I found out that he has relatives on a farm near here. Maybe he'll go there before starting on the trip to New Orleans with Jim.

My plan is to help Jim escape before they set out for New Orleans. Once he gets to town, you and I can step in and buy his freedom for him.

That's a great idea, Tom. I'm with you.

Tom was right, Jim's master took him to a farm, not far away, where . . .

Cousin Hunter! What brings you here?

Hello, Billy, I hope you won't mind if I spend the night. Tomorrow I'll take the stage coach for New Orleans.

Put this boy in safekeeping. I've had to travel like crazy to find him.

I understand. The boy is your property. Don't worry, he won't escape.

After dark . . .
Let's get closer. Wherever they have Jim locked up, he'll hear our signal.

Will we be able to get him out of here, Tom?

And then Tom gave the secret signal of his gang. All the boys knew that sound.

MEOW! MEE O WW!

The sheets are gone! I put them on the line to dry this morning!

Grab the line, before someone sees us!

Oh, the sheets are gone!

Emmalina, there hasn't been a bit of wind. I'll go with you to see . . .

Hurry, Jim, hurry! Someone's coming!

What could have happened? Are you sure you hung them out?

Yes, Ma'am. I put them out.

Well, that's what you say, but . . . Oh, no!

He's escaping! The little black boy is escaping!

Did you hear? My slave . . .

Hurry!

He went that way. There were two other boys with him.

We've got to get to the river before they're on top of us!

Tom Sawyer's plan did not include a boat. Instead . . .

But minutes later . . .

Okay, they're gone. The danger is over.

Never again! Never again in the water!

Don't you think that you had a nice bath, Jim? No kidding. Ha, ha! I do!

It did you good, Jim.

Okay fellas, back to town. It's time we went home.

Wait, Tom!

We have to be careful when we get there. Have you forgotten that everyone thinks I'm dead? If Mrs. Douglas sees me suddenly, she might just die of fright!

Don't worry, Huck. I have a plan.

Jim and I will speak to her. We'll explain how your father forced you to go to that cabin with him and how he tried to get his hands on the money.

Never again! Never!

That's enough grumbling, Jim. You should thank Tom for what he's done for you. He followed your old master when he showed up in town looking for you. So Tom was able to save you.

You're right, Huck. I was being selfish.

Thanks, Tom. If it weren't for you, I'd have ended up in New Orleans.

It's nothing. When we get to town, Huck and I will buy your freedom with our money.

During that scene of deep friendship, Jim's eyes filled with tears of joy and gratitude.

I'll never forget you and Huck!

The next day, late in the afternoon..

Anything new about Huck Finn, Sheriff?

Nothing. The poor boy must have been drowned in the river by the thieves who captured him.

After the fourth funeral service that Mrs. Douglas had held in memory of her godchild . . .

What do you think? What do you think could really have happened?

They'll find out, Miss Dorothy.

Poor boy! Poor boy!

Poor Mrs. Douglas. Isn't it awful about her sadness, Miss Pattibush?

He was like a son to her, Miss Dorothy

Aaaaw!

Boy, how are we going to explain all this to the good Mrs. Douglas?

But no explanation was necessary because the good woman saw the "ghost" at once . . .

Huck, my son!

She loved the boy so much that all she could do was . . .

Mrs. Douglas!

Thank goodness! In spite of what everyone said, I felt you were alive, Huck!

Tom Sawyer told all he knew, starting with the time Huck's father took Huck from town. The next day in the sheriff's office...

And Huck and I want to use the money they gave us as a reward that time for finding the robbers' loot . . .

to buy Jim's freedom. That's it, Sheriff.

That's a great thing to do, boys. And you, Jim, will be freed forever from being a slave.

Tell me, Miss Pattibush. Was it really a ghost? I don't understand it at all!

Neither do I!

THE END